MW00441734

TEA LEAF READING

Dennis Fairchild

RUNNING PRESS
PHILADELPHIA

Running Press
Hachette Book Group
1290 Avenue of the Americas, New York, NY 10104
www.runningpress.com
@Running_Press

Printed in China

First Edition: September 2015

Published by Running Press, an imprint of Perseus Books, LLC, a subsidiary of Hachette Book Group, Inc. The Running Press name and logo is a trademark of the Hachette Book Group.

The Hachette Speakers Bureau provides a wide range of authors for speaking events. To find out more, go to www.hachettespeakersbureau.com or call (866) 376-6591.

The publisher is not responsible for websites (or their content) that are not owned by the publisher.

Library of Congress Control Number: 2015933753

ISBN: 978-0-7624-5640-6

TLF

11 10 9 8 7 6 5 4 3

Table of Contents

I read the tea leaves
as if they were words
left over from a conversation
between two cups.
-Kenny Knight,
The Honicknowle Book of the Dead

YOU ARE NOW ENTERING

*Tea-Leaf Reading
Bootcamp*

Each cup of tea represents
an imaginary voyage.

~C. Douzel

Good news! Learning how to read tea leaves in a cup, like sentences in a book, has never been easier or more thirst-quenching. The bad news is that you'll never be able to look at a cup of tea the same way, ever again.

This book isn't simply a collection of first-time reveals and secret step-by-step instructions on how to tease and squeeze information about the future out of wet things in the bottom of teacups. It's also your personal invite to a most unique tea party where perceptions are of the extrasensory sort and all talk is about the future. Thirsty for more? Grab a teacup, close the refrigerator door, turn on the kettle, and open up your mind.

For instant wisdom and intuitive insights, just add water!

Tea-Reading History

England a fortune-telling host,
As num'rous as the stars, could boast;
Matrons, who toss the cup, and see
The grounds of Fate in grounds of tea . . .
~C. Churchill

The Japanese, Chinese, Aborigine, African, and Eastern and American Indians—some of the world's oldest and most spiritual cultures—believe that every flower talks and all rocks breathe. Many global cultures accept that everything is "alive" and vibrates with its own personal energies, including every herb and twig. Sometime around 350 AD, somewhere in China, somebody developed the teachings of tasseomancy or tassology, a.k.a., tea-leaf reading. "Tasse" is an ancient Eastern word, meaning small cup or goblet. Asian, Greek, and Middle East royalty adored the tall tales from their teacups and it quickly became popular, especially among the movers and shakers of the upper class.

Today, every culture on the planet has their own how-to venue to translate teacup symbols. Interestingly, every twist, brand, and version has more in common with one another, than differences.

Like cutting a deck of tarot cards, tea-leaf interpretation operates on the Law of Attraction philosophy and ancient symbols: What may appear in a cup as random clumps of tea leaves is actually a precise arrangement that forms the answers and insights to the tea drinker's concerns. The aim of this little book is to demystify ancient arcane tea-talk into mellow modern lingo. Cheers!

Before the Water Boils . . .

If you are cold, tea will warm you.
If you are too heated, it will cool you.
If you are depressed, it will cheer you.
If you are excited, it will calm you.

-W. E. Gladstone

The medicinal, magical qualities of earth's herbs and flowers are rich with ancient lore and history. At some point, every piece of shrub and tree bark on the planet has taken a turn getting thrown into a dark, jungle-hot prison filled with boiling water, then hung out to dry and discarded—all in the name of tuning in to "the future."

Authentic contemporary tea-leaf readers have nothing to do with modern-day tea "bags." Granted, teabags leave a cup squeaky clean and brew a tasty drink, but they're not suited for leaf reading. In addition to infusing the sipping experience with more flavor, aroma, antioxidants, and pleasure than mass-produced teabags, whole-leaf tea "leaves" more distinct letters and symbols in the cup.

The mindful and professional

tea-leaf reader uses organic loose leaf tea leaves only—no additives or fake flavors, please. Chemically treated tea leaves make chemical tea. Period. Choose wisely.

Which tea will give you the "best" reading, you ask? Chinese green teas and oolong varieties are tailor-made for the curious tea-leaf reader. Both feature pliant leaves of various lengths, which makes for a more distinct and detailed image in the cup. If you're just starting out: Go green!

At one time or another, every culture on this planet has experimented with exotic, herbal, and floral tea ceremonies as a means to enhance psychic powers and "see" the future. Legends record that the Oracle at Delphi supplemented her clairvoyant visions by chewing bay leaves. Like in centuries past, today's clairvoyants and crystal-ball readers (a.k.a. "scryers") regard tea brewed from the leaves of the mugwort plant as the best, drinkable e.s.p.-catalyst on the planet.

Dedicated tea-leaf readers give two pinky fingers-up to Darjeeling, the "Champagne of tea." This premium tea's distinctive color, aroma, and flavor mimics a fine muscatel and is attributed to its otherworldly Himalayan Mountain roots, 7,000-feet above the northeastern corner of India. Darjeeling makes for a fine cup of tea, and very good tea leaf reading.

Treat yourself to a road trip down the tea aisle of your local supermarket or health food store and do some grazing and taste testing. Investigate tea's vast healing and metaphysical properties with the help of your computer's search engine and surf online tea sellers for free samples. Loose-leaf and bagged teas should be stored in airtight containers away from direct sunlight. It's also a smart idea to consult your doctor before experimenting with any herbal substance.

Let's Get This Tea-Party Started . . .

"Would you like an adventure now . . .
or would you like to have your tea first?"
Wendy quickly replied: "tea first."
-J.M. Barrie, *Peter Pan*

Doing a tea-leaf reading is as simple as boiling water—which is where we begin. Because a cup of tea is 99 percent water, the purer the water, the finer your final brew and happier your spirit. Ingredient-wise: nature and natural rule. Avoid using tap water.

A stainless steel kettle is the one of choice amongst tea-readers. Go for stovetop kettles, not electric ones with bothersome cords. Also, it's a smart idea to have available a small number of teaspoons, for cup-swirling and poking at the leaves. All tea utensils must be stainless steel or sterling silver. To keep the stars on your tea party's side, astrology favors using silver or stainless steel utensils, exclusively—both are psychic-generating moon-related metals. Aluminum and plastic items should be avoided.

EVERYBODY SING:

I'm a Little Teapot

Water is the mother of tea;
a teapot its father and fire the teacher.
-Chinese adage

A small 2-cup, 20-ounce teapot makes the best tea and clearest fortunes.

Choose a teapot that pours easily, doesn't drip when tilted, and whose spout allows the leaves to flow freely into the cup when you pour. Peek inside the pot and examine any built-in "strainer" between the body of the bowl and the spout. Choose a teapot whose interior colander-like holes are big enough to allow plenty of tea leaves to flow down the spout's snout.

Ceramic and stone teapots are preferred by smart, contemporary tea-reading schools. Dense ceramic pots hold heat longer and promote better brewing. Have nothing to do with aluminum ones or pots with built-in electric cords that plug into wall sockets. Go for round and ball-like teapots, not long or square. (Plus, round pots are easier to clean.)

To produce full-bodied flavor, tea leaves need room to expand and stretch. The shape of a round pot encourages tea leaves to swirl and twirl and unfurl easily and gently, encouraging lush tea symbols. A good teapot also features a vented lid that doesn't fall out of the pot when poured and a heat-resistant handle with ample room between the handle and the pot's lid.

The Teacup: Plain or Fancy?

Time to choose your cup and saucer. Cup first. Be mindful of the selection process; don't rush. Pick the cup up. Touch it. Hold it. Curl your hands around it. Grip it by the handle—how's it feel?

Teacup color and embellishments are of no consequence. However, cups with white or light ivory interiors—like pages in a new book—make for a more pleasant tea read. Choose a cup with a wide, round, spacious bowl, so your brewing artsy tea leaves can swim around and fly freely within. Go for a cup with a firm handle—a solid, strong-looking one—not dainty or fragile. Forego mugs and straight-sided glasses.

The cup's saucer is also a vital component in tea-leaf prognostication, acting as a "file cabinet" for extraneous bits and pieces of loose-leaf leftovers. Select a saucer that's approximately two times wider than the mouth of the

cup, with a raised rimmed circumfer-
ence for catching and containing drips
and irrelevant verbiage. Your teacup
does not have to match your saucer.
Lastly, keep some attractive absorbent
napkins nearby for spills and wet, run-
away tea leaves.

Ready to Roil?

We had a kettle: we let it leak:
Our not repairing it made it worse.
We haven't had any tea for a week . . .
The bottom is out of the Universe!

-R. Kipling

Please note: Each guest drinks from their own 2-cup teapot and uses their own teacup. No sharing—lest ye dare share another's fate and karma!

Meander over to the sink, fill the kettle with 4 to 5 cups of cold water and heat on the stovetop. As soon as the water reaches a boil, turn off the burner and quickly fill your pre-selected 2-cup teapot. Warm the pot for 33 seconds, then recycle the water.

Never boil the tea in the pot or kettle! Tea is delicate and scorched tea leaves will result in a bitter tasting tea (and an unappetizing fortune). The longer water is boiled, the less oxygen it contains. Oxygen in the water is what releases the leaves' flavor.

Now, into the bottom of your newly warm teapot, spoon 3 teaspoons of loose tea. Then spoon 1 teaspoon of loose leaf tea into each cup, plus 1 for the pot.

Cover the leaves with 2 cups of hot, but not boiling, water. The ballet-like movements that tea leaves make after hot water is poured over is called "the agony of the leaves."

By the by, if you prefer your tea with sugar, place the sugar in your teapot before adding the tea leaves and boiling water for a more accurate reading—never add sugar to a fully-brewed cup. Bottoms up!

THE RITUAL SWIRL:
Third Time's a Charm

Each cup represents an
imaginary voyage.
~C. Douzel

Time to put the Art Critic Hat on your head and sneak a peek at what's happening inside your teacup. If your teacup doesn't have any or many tea leaves in it, don't fret—use a teaspoon to scoop some from the bottom of the teapot and place them in the bottom of your cup. Then, stir gently.

Now, before you start sipping, hold your teacup in your hand of choice and slowly move the cup in front of you in a circular, counter-clockwise motion, three times. If you're uncomfortable by this technique, choose to discreetly stir your brew with a teaspoon in three counter-clockwise circles instead.

Mystery Schools consider three a magical number, denoting something special. For example, the saying, "third time's a charm" encourages you to put recent disappointment aside and try, try again. Three hand-held spins of the cup, symbolically "separates" the past and present from the future, acting like a psychic centrifuge, making it easier to distinguish what's passed and what's up for the tea drinker.

Most importantly: Take time to relax your mind and enjoy your tea! Close your eyes and inhale its aromatic warmth. Note all thoughts and random words that pop into your mind and let them go. Take a deep breath. Hold it for a second or two. Exhale, open your eyes, and start sipping your tea. Don't think of anything while you're drinking. Allow your mind to wander and flutter.

And please don't drain every last drop from your cup. Leave a small amount of liquid in the bottom of your cup—less than a teaspoon—to swirl around and help the tea leaves "paint" their symbols on the cup's interior.

Next, with your favored hand, swirl your near-empty teacup three times in a counter-clockwise circular direction, wetting the inner bowl with moist leaves. Now formulate a question in your mind about the future. Got it?

Lastly, turn your cup over onto your saucer in one quick, solid motion, and let the remaining moisture drip out for a couple of minutes. (Do you remember where you put those absorbent napkins?) For best results and accuracy, "read" only from the first cup poured; recycle any remaining liquid.

THE TEACUP'S
PSYCHIC SYMBOLS:

Is That Blob an Elephant or an Ant?

Enjoy life sip by sip, not gulp by gulp.
-The Ministry of Leaves

After emptying most of the leftover liquid into your saucer, take a slow, sideways looksee at the squiggles and blobs spread around the interior of your cup. Note all blatantly familiar objects created by the leaves and tea-twigs. Be patient. Like seeing in the dark, spotting a symbol may require a moment or two for your eyes to adjust. Don't worry if you don't spot something familiar immediately. Initially, most patterns appear by "happenstance," before assuming a specific appearance or meaning.

Don't pressure, push, or punish yourself to see something in the leaves either. Like gazing in the sky for patterns in clouds, eventually you'll see "something." And that's when the Sacred Symbols Glossary joins the tea-party.

"Magic" symbols? Well, yes. A symbol is "something that represents something else by association, resemblance or con-vention; especially, a material object used to represent something invisible." A symbol always represents something more than its obvious meaning—some-thing *invisible* in that we cannot totally define it. That's quite magical, wouldn't you agree?

A symbol can represent more than one thing. When you're uncertain what you think you're seeing, hone your intu-ition by simply following your first gut feeling. By relaxing, breathing deeply, and being really quiet, you will "hear" your intuitive Inner Voice. First, in whispers, then getting louder and clearer with every future cup of tea. Intuitive flashes spring unpredictably from the unconscious—from out of the void, as it were. And, in this case, from those wet blobs of tea in your cup.

Tea Time

✳

This morning's tea
makes yesterday distant.
~Tanko

Tea-leaf symbols reveal clues about who, what, where, and why.

"When" hints are told by where in the teacup the symbol is located. It's all up/down and right/left from here on. "Reading" time is very easy once you understand the basic "map" of the teacup.

With your mind's eye, divide the teacup's interior into three concentric

sections—like a three-ringed target—
with the largest, widest circle devot-
ed to the cup's upper-third and rim
(representing future times), and the
smallest "bullseye" section in bottom
(suggesting shadows and conflicts of
the distant past).

- Symbols in the cup's lower-third tell
of conflicts and circumstances of the
recent past, influences that are behind
you, but may still weigh on your

shoulders. The teacup's bottom-third whispers of secrets and days gone by and is named Sector 1.

- Above, the circular middle-third symbolizes the present, what's popping or plopping on the front burner. Symbols in the left-side of the cup's circular middle-third suggest recent opportunities and circumstances. Current matters are the middle-third area's concern and is called Sector 2.

• Future happenings are forecasted by the leaves in the top upper-third and rim of the teacup. Here, what's right around the corner is found in the circular upper-area of the cup, dubbed Sector 3. Images closest to the rim in the right-side of this section suggest the near future.

Which symbol gets analyzed first, you ask? Start with the one that first catches your eye and you keep coming back for another look. Or, begin with the biggest shape. Like life, there's no set in stone protocol. Let your eyes and your imagination glide and flutter across the cup's landscape and note what inhabits where. Meander and wander from leaf to leaf, clump to clump, symbol to symbol. Remember: Tea-advice is always hopeful, healthy, and helpful.

Over the centuries, many tea-predicting secrets have gotten muddled and lost in translations. Today's tea-leaf readers believe that you don't need to know exactly where your life is ultimately going. What you need is to recognize the possibilities and challenges offered by the present moment and to embrace them with courage and faith. Now, congratulate yourself for how far you've come and go enjoy a good tea-read.

How to Read Between the Lines . . . Rather, The Leaves

Where there's tea, there's hope.
-A. W. Pinero

Agreed: A rose is a rose is a rose. However, when seen in a teacup and made from wet globs of leaves and twigs, it's not likely for it to look *exactly* like the ones in grandma's garden. Open up your third eye and unleash your imagination—and consult the Symbol Glossary!

✦⟨⟨⟨⟩⟩⟩ A ⟨⟨⟨⟩⟩⟩✦

The **acorn** symbolizes slow, steady movement; prudence and patience. Line up ducks, fine-tune plans. In Sectors 2 and 3: good news about long-term investments—financial, as well as familial ones. Sector 1: forget old grudges, but remember past setbacks. Be purposeful.

Be footloose and willing to leave the past behind and take a few leaps of faith, signals the **airplane**. Any Sector: Travel goes well. Escape toxic noise, pushy people. Welcome fresh and out-of-the-blue experiences. In Sectors 1 and 2: company arrives; changes in the household. Hack away at the unessential.

The **boat anchor** says slow down, take time to smell the water lilies. Keep matters uncomplicated, logical. Any Sector: not the time for action; better for brainstorming, handling one thing at a time.

Travel plans delayed. Upright-pointing anchor prongs: Help is offered to you; downward pointing: You're on your own; go solo.

~62~

Angels are omens of happy news, renewed interest. In Sector 1: Rewards from previous efforts arrive; favorable news of pregnancy. In Sectors 2 and 3: wholesome escape; home improvement; return to vitality. Kiss and make up; reunion with loved ones; a time of tithing. Give yourself permission to grow stronger and brighter at your own pace. Worry less, live longer.

❊

Ants (or bugs in general) imply busyness; time is money. Health obstacles diminish. In Sector 1: Help is on the way/was offered; need for teamwork. Give it all you've got! In Sector 2 and 3: Don't imitate what has always worked before; be willing to depart from the script.

The **apple** is a symbol of achievement, growth, and prosperity. As it was in Eden, the apple promotes risk-taking, breaking protocol; change. Keep playing to your strengths and emphasizing what you love. Recognize the possibilities and challenges offered by the present moment, when in Sector 2. In Sector 3: luck with law; contracts, leases, and legal work favored.

An **arch** (like an upside-down letter

"U,") signals growth and expansion; help from peers; future honor and recognition; a healthy, new financial opportunity. Slow and steady progress. In Sectors 2 and 3: Call for courage, faith, and hope. Don't over-extend/exhaust yourself. In Sector 3: A change of scenery, vacation, improves health and wealth.

⚔

An **arrow** calls for cleverness and reveals fast-paced and frustrating times. Travel goes well; welcome visitors. Sectors 1 and 2: important details overlooked, slight deception; budget; team or partner's game plan not realistic. Sector 3 or near cup handle: favorable changes for loved ones; a sensual time; unexpected windfall. Luck comes when you maintain the highest standards of ethical behavior.

The **axe** is a protective voice of reason that warns against verbal conflicts and disagreements. In Sector 1 the worst is over; good triumphs over bad. Declare your independence from schedule; depart from the itinerary. Sectors 2 and 3: Keep your own counsel, be quiet; go solo; tell yourself the truth about what's going on.

❈❈❈ B ❈❈❈

The **ball**—a filled-in, round circle, like a polka-dot (not an open "O") symbolizes healthy escapism; greener social pastures; travel. In Sector 1: Help is offered; weakness, poor vitality. Sector 2 increases the tempo, prompting change of residence, movement; work load increasing. Sector 3: Success from the past, collect outstanding debts; help/acknowledgement from professionals.

*

A **basket** (like a waste basket) warns of extravagance, weak investments, and slow financial times when in Sector 1; financial deception and letdown from partners/friends in Sector 2. Sector 3 represents improved health; beware of weight gain. Upgrade home furnishings; luck with real estate; health improves; weight loss.

A **bat** image calls for more investigating and reviewing; warns of being sidetracked by peripheral concerns. In all Sectors: chill out; vacation; a time for reflection, retreat, and meditation. Compete with no one but yourself. Read between the lines and look beneath the surface. In Sector 3: sponsorship; recognition; public buzz.

When the **bell** appears, it's a wake-up call—seek compromise; roll up your sleeves and be ready to do your part; consider the greater good. Nurture your mind with confident thoughts and be willing to ask for help. In Sectors 1 and 3: news of poor health; test-taking and credentials excel; brilliant news from afar. In Sector 2: health improves; sales go well; need for personal private vacation or retreat.

A **bird** in flight with open wings indicates a change of course/direction; a healthy escape. In any sector: Don't sugarcoat matters; keep promises to yourself. One or two birds in one Sector is favorable; three or more suggest loss of personal freedom beware of bullies.

An open **book** (resembling a relaxed letter "V") highlights social occasions and career opportunity. Any Sector: It's time to create a niche that's tailored to your specific talents and needs. Sector 2: time to move in another direction; next phase. Sector 3: luck from law and education; better time to invest, not withdraw.

Traditionally, one or more silhouettes of long-necked wine or soda **bottles** in any

Sector suggests exhaustion; the need to relax and escape from unhealthy environments. The body is fragile. Slow down; digest what's happening around you. Take your time; don't hurry.

A **bridge** (resembling a dash or long hyphen) shouts "move forward;" favorable travel. Sector 1: reunions; good news about long ago. Sector 2: Luck arrives when you depart from the script. Don't rest on laurels or past achievements. Sector 3: Cooperative business ventures go well.

❋

A **bowl** (like the letter "U") asks you to take your time, slow down, and enjoy improved health. Sector 1: While home and love interests are on the up and up, beware of gossip, malice. Sectors 2 and 3: favorable change in funds from the outside. Tweak your own karma.

❋

The **broom** is a favorable omen of

personal change. A busy, active time; beware of over-extending yourself. Insist on the real thing. Sectors 1 and 2: new beginnings; brighter attitude; independence. Sector 3: new friendships; tipsters; social opportunities expand.

※

The **butterfly**, like the angel, brings a return of self-esteem, happiness, positive news. Changes in associates and family; out with the old. Time to quiet any critical dialogue you're having with yourself about what you perceive as your "shortcomings." Sectors 2 and 3: home improvement. Demonstrate how much power you have to understand and cope with the changes that need changing.

❧ C ❧

The **candle** is all about taking your time, emphasizing inner health and beauty; fortitude; self-improvement.

Sector 1: wisdom through isolation; tests and exams; improve immature skills. Sectors 2 and 3: acknowledgement from peers; luck arrives when doing what you don't do very well.

❧

A **car** (like, a rectangle on wheels) shouts "stop, look, and listen!" In any Sector: a necessary and urgent need to clear the air; unhealthy escapism. Sector 2: Beware of new associates, latest deals. Sector 3: out-of-sync; change of plans; delays. Compete with no one but yourself.

❦

The **chair** is all about personal progress, your true-blue support system. In any Sector: favorable news from old friends; luck from what you already have; a socially quiet time. Sector 2: de-clutter; wriggle free of any ruts you've been stuck in. Sector 3: new friends; promotion looms; possible weight gain.

A round, open **circle** signifies improved health and vigor; fertility. Change your mind about the world. A time of evangelizing; egos. Sectors 1 and 2: surgery; pregnancy; real estate news. Sector 3: additional source of income; profits grow from unlearning and deprograming; fresh imaginings.

A **clover** (3- or 4-leaf) reassures that secrets are safe and confidentiality respected. Sector 1: details of private trips; social intrigue. Home improvement; news of company, from Sector 2. Back every speech, gesture, and action with a concentrated wealth of meaning, says Sector 3. Real estate favored.

✄

A hair **comb** encourages individual thinking and action; going solo. Ask questions, don't presume. Sector 1 and 2: news of love; beware of gossip. Sector 3: secrets bring smiles; pamper yourself. Celebrate what you want to see more of.

Accept new assistance and support for your concerns when a **comet** with its tail appears in Sectors 2 or 3. A slow time financially; better for planning than action. Delays in plans reveal favorable hidden clues. Have nothing to do with gossip. Sector 1: out-with-the-old; loss of friendship; minor, fleeting blemish to reputation.

The **cross** (or, "+" sign) signals a time of rest, peace. Victory, after much inner-suffering and sacrifice. Sector 1: inheritance; news of children; parental concerns. In Sectors 2 and 3: solitude; independent travel; following much struggle, improved personal health and happiness.

A **crown** tells of achievement; lucrative investments; profit. In Sector 1: loans repaid; sales go well. Sector 2: respect from others; moving forward. Sector 3: independent activity favored; personal rewards and indulgence. Health on upswing.

🌿

An upright **cup** (tea or coffee) denotes: "take your time, think a bit longer." Dance to your own soundtrack. No rushing allowed; a call for meditation; weigh out pros and cons. In Sector 1: long-distance travel or visitors. In Sectors 2 and 3: a well-deserved break; vacation.

🌿

A **dagger** (bigger than a butter knife and shorter than a sword) urges you to remove the unnecessary; houseclean "friends;" de-clutter. Bullying is possible, in Sectors 1 and 3. Sector 2 favors athletes and health care.

❧

The **diamond** gives gifts to the drama-free. Appearing in Sectors 1 and 2 begs you to slow down, weigh out options. Good for brainstorming, education, and buying (not selling). An encouraging prompt for weight loss, new lovers in Sector 3.

A **dot**, or series of them, denotes deception over money; financial schemes. In any Sector: All is not as it appears on the surface. For best results, brainstorm with professionals; seek expert advice. A series of dots in Sectors 1 and 2 warn about busy-bodies, yet delivers group support. In Sector 3: luck from government; rewards from educational or health facility.

❊❊❊ E ❊❊❊

An **egg** tells of improved health; new opportunities; fertility. Projects growing a healthy, proper manner. Sector 1 warns of broken personal promises; disappointments over family. In Sectors 2 and 3: acknowledgement, input, and proposals from outside sources—realize how much power you have to change anything you want to change.

※

An **evergreen** is the symbol for inner-strength, fortitude, and standing your ground. Shine your light brightly. In Sectors 1 and 2: status quo regarding health; repetition and routine rules. Sector 3 says let history and common sense help you cut through any illusions that have been hurting you.

※

Exclamation points warn of family

conflicts, domestic conflicts, and arguments with friends. In whichever Sector: don't get hung up by criticism or naysayers. Be braver and bolder in expressing yourself. Sector 2 says reconnect with nature; relax; de-stress. In terms of business, in Sector 3: say "no," when necessary; approach situations obliquely, at an angle.

✳

The **eye** warns of deception; theft;

one-upmanship. Have another looksee. In Sectors 2 and 3: Break free from
claustrophobic situations and people.
Facts not clear; have another think;
keep a back-up plan handy. Same reading, when eyeglasses appear.

⚔️ F ⚔️

A hand-held **fan** warns of temporary
happiness; fleeting flirtation; self-
deception. Not seeing the entire pic-
ture. Intimidation from loved ones in

Sector 1. Sector 2 suggests holding off; bide your time. Tend to any old wounds or frightening beliefs that might be interfering with where you want to be, says Sector 3.

Fish represent prosperity, peace, and contentment. Give yourself permission to grow stronger and brighter. In Sectors 1 and 3: improved health; happy household. Sector 2: victory against outside interference; reject all actions that demoralize and hurt.

❀

A **fishhook** reveals disagreements; compromise; the need for more thinking. In Sector 1: family health crisis; minor accident. Sector 2 warns of unrealistic financial plans; unprofitable business talks. Unleash your inner detective. Say "no" without explaining yourself.

❀

A **flag** waving warns to pay more attention to individual parts and beneath-the-surface details. Tears over broken promises, when in Sector 1. Sector 2 and 3 highlights unrealistic business propositions; time-wasting endeavors. However, travel and recreational pursuits go well, in Sector 3.

One **flying bird**, or a **flock**, speaks of successful experimenting; slipping free from ruts; self-expression. In Sectors 1 and 2: Important messages free you from worry; cull outworn friendships. Sector 3: travel; avoid repetition: Don't get pinned down or forced to be consistent.

✄

One **flower**—like a daisy or tulip—symbolizes new love (in the form of a person); renewed affection. Two flowers signify monogamous love affair. Attention and warm gifts arrive in Sector 2. Good for big ticket item purchasing in Sector 3.

✄

A **foot** calls for controlled, precise, in-the-moment focus. Contract renewal; higher education. In Sector 1: tradition and protocol broken; family hassles; conflict. Escape the noise and crowds, travel in Sector 2; and, keep distance from rash dares in Sector 3.

The **fork** (like a trident, or the letter "Y") warns of vague and questionable proposals; stalemate; indecision. A time to undo, dismantle, and disperse. Sector

1 and 2: Go with logic and tradition, the tried-and-true. Sector 3 favors adventure, increases intuition and instincts; go for the "new"; stay in control.

The **gun** (pistol or rifle) calls for reason and logic, not erratic behavior. In Sector 1: parent-child conflict; familial upset; arguments and door-slamming. Sector 2 calls for diplomacy; second opinions; business quarrels.

Sector 3: Control your karma; turn your cheek; walk away; cut your losses. Curb mischievousness; stick to the familiar.

The **hammer** is about physical energy and strength; athletic victory; fertility/virility. In any Sector: a return to health; renewed strength and resources. Sector 1: home improvement; luxury item purchase; legacies. Sectors 2: Keep your own counsel; think twice before acting. Sector 3: projects completed; business concludes. Take the high road.

A **hand** with fingers spread accepts help from friends; change of scenery; luck from new activities (and extra money when in Sector 3). Any Sector: tension subsides; favors received. Sector 3 favors high standards, credentials; loans; purchases.

A **hand mirror** speaks of second opinions; stick with the reliable and familiar. Tend to old wounds. Not a time for radical change or going solo. Sector 2 increases social life and applause; shower blessings on your vulnerabilities. In Sector 3: Wise advice arrives; collect debts. Observe before you engage.

❦

A man's **hat**—like a top hat, or gentleman's bowler—speaks of awards and honor; the kindness of strangers;

applause; recognition from peers. Sectors 1 and 2: You're being taken seriously; luck from elders. Sector 3: luck from new faces; new places; travel; help from afar.

*

The **horizon** (a line with sunrise/sunset, or house or tree, on top) says take a vacation; escape; lighten up; stop fretting over matters that don't really matter much in the big scheme. In any Sector: Playtime is favored over work and finances. Sector 1:

concern for another's health; winning compromise. Sector 3: favors granted; inheritance. Protest dullness and celebrate what you want to see more of!

An **hourglass** brings optimistic news of reunions, friends from afar. "Time" is on your side; improved health. Sectors 1 and 2: busy social time. Sector 3 favors education, loans, favors gained. Like its image suggests: Stay in the moment and make every minute count.

Don't overreact how others treat you. At this time, it's more important how you treat them.

✱

A **house** reveals one's yearning for inner stability and peace of mind. Sectors 1 and 2: ongoing family concerns; news of pregnancy; not a time for socializing. Sector 3: relocation; personal retreat; convalescing improves. Accept every person and every situation on its own terms.

❈❘❘❘❘❘ J ❘❘❘❘❘❈

Jail bars (a barred window) warn of anemic economic times; exhaustion and depression. Are you settling for too little? Expecting too much? Sectors 1 and 2 lessen the intensity of worry. Watch your step. Seek professional help in Sector 3—you're not thinking clearly. Worry less, live longer.

❈❘❘❘❘❘ K ❘❘❘❘❘❈

A **key** represents an escape from

restrictions; new horizons. In any Sector: Heed the advice of natives, professionals, and elders. Sector 1: confidential plans; "old" money; financial secrets. Sectors 2 and 3: economic recovery via new friendships. Reward what you like and pursue what you want and let others to do the same.

The **keyhole** represents fresh opportunities; choice and decision time. Maintain confidences; leave the past behind.

Don't rush to judgment. Sectors 2 and 3: New faces bring profit.

❦

The **kite**—flying with a string and tail or not—is tea leaf reading's Aladdin's lamp and classic symbol for personal happiness. Sweep aside exhausting and distracting worries. Sectors 1 and 2: Be more curious and open-minded; travel goes well. Sector 3 applauds and assists long-distance relationships.

❦

A **knife** (shorter than a sword) urges professional intervention/involvement; the need for objective advice. Emotional conflict on the rise; patience and thick skin required. Sector 1: unfinished family business; jilted lovers. Sectors 2 warns of deceit with new associates; short trips favored, not long journeys. Draw on others' own hard-won epiphanies.

 L

A **ladder** symbolizes financial growth,

smart financial opportunities and decisions. A ladder with four or more rungs tells of inheritance. Short trips favored. The cavalry arrives; accept all tips and helping hands. Make room for fresh imaginings.

A **leaf**—or a small number of them—say go with the innovative and the new. In any Sector: warm and wonderful changes; more personal financial freedom. In Sector 1: out with the old brings luck; bury the past. Sector 3: review/refresh love status. Don't think in terms of limitations.

🦋

Letters of the alphabet may signify names of family or business associates, future loves or pals. When intuiting from a specific letter, follow your gut's first feeling.

🦋

A **lightning bolt** speeds up closure and endings and calls for action. Expand,

push forward and reach out. A time
of improved vitality and healthy family news in Sector 1. Business-finan-
cial stalemates mellow in Sectors 2
and 3 thanks to flashes of inspiration.
Unleash your freest freewill.

A **lock** warns of stalemate; obstacles,
the need to re-plan. In any Sector: not a
time of action. Be mindful of stubborn-
ness, close-mindedness, and prejudice.
Discard anything that worries and

weakens you at this time. Have nothing
to do with it.

✳✳✳✳✳✳ M ✳✳✳✳✳✳

A **magnifying glass** says stick with
the reliable and familiar; don't go to
extremes. Ask for favors; admit faults;
learn secrets. Sector 2: important
health news; shower blessings on the
elderly. In Sector 3: good for revamp-
ing and reviewing; collecting debts.
Observe before you engage.

A superhero-like **mask** warns of secret-keeping and gossip; withheld facts. In any Sector, a respectful need for confidentiality, quiet, and privacy prevails. Not the time for getting facts or asking for loans and favors. Welcome partial successes and useless mistakes

✳

A **crescent moon** (waxing or waning) tells of emotional sharing and inter-personal interaction. Don't mistake feelings with facts. Sector 2 warn of emotional duplicity or blackmail; domestic stalemate; foggy and flirtatious. The heart is messing with the head. Bark less, bless more.

A **mouse** is a sign of slow, improving health and temporary freedom from physical restrictions, but warns of deception when in Sector 1. Independent thinking and acting preferred. Budget, review, and think twice; facts aren't on the bargaining table yet.

A **mountain** or **mountain range** predicts success after much struggle. Be alert to details and fine print. In Sectors 2 and 3: Reconsider offers of help and others' advice. Strength in numbers. Sector 3: personal success; another chance to try again and do it better. Congratulate yourself for how far you've come.

The **mushroom**, a classic symbol for patience, says slow down, relax, and digest what's happening around you. In

Sectors 1 and 2: not a time for action, speculation, or travel. Befriend your blood pressure. Recognize the possibilities and challenges of the moment and embrace them with faith, courage, and hope.

A **musical note** sings of peaceful times and love affairs; marriages and pregnancy. Tell yourself the truth about what's going on. Sectors 2 and 3: new home furnishings; breakthrough in therapy; spiritual revelations.

✵⟨⟨⟨⟨ O ⟩⟩⟩⟩✵

An **oval** or **open circle** denotes self-improvement; health and vitality returns. In Sectors 1: personal getaway; private epiphany. Sector 2: new business associate or teacher. Sectors 2 and 3: favorable medical news; family turbulence subsides.

✵⟩⟩⟩⟩ P ⟨⟨⟨⟨✵

A **palm tree** signifies travel and warns of fly-by-night schemes; change of unclear plans. Remove yourself from idiots and others' approval. Not a good time to negotiate contracts/finances. Luck for domestic pets.

※

A **pen** or **pencil** signals the need for a jury of peers; get a second opinion; facts are one-sided. Sector 1: important email or letter. Sectors 2 and 3: better for sales than purchases. Keep everything on the high road.

※

Like an exclamation point, the **pyramid** shouts something's up and it won't get any rest until it's taken care of. Loss of privacy. A better time for discovery not debate. Go for facts. Flaws in written agreements uncovered. Changes in travel plans.

❧ Q ❧

A **question mark** warns of clutter and confusion; absurd priorities. Any Sector: Get things in writing. Unusual gifts

Changes and delays in plans bring good fortune. Sector 2: weary; over-extended. Rest rather than work.

✲✲✲✲✲✲ R ✲✲✲✲✲✲

The **rabbit** speaks of independent activity and personal bravery. Break from routine. Health victory. Sector 1: changes in household members. Sectors 2 and 3: real estate news; short trip. Luck.

No running away from problems, says
the **sailboat**. Sectors 1 and 2: Luck
comes from neighborhood and home;
reunions. Sector 3: social times; an
end to loneliness. Cut yourself the
slack you need.

Scissors symbolize unfinished plans
and half-baked schemes. Read between
the lines; be patient. Others may not
have your best interests in mind.

Whether evenly balanced or not, **scales** warn of unfair play; disagreements and white lies. Immaturity. Sectors 1 and 2: faulty mechanical equipment; separation, divorce.

The **shoe** emphasizes speed and vitality; convalescing. A positive symbol of forward movement; relief from boredom. Leisure and pleasure travel goes well. Sectors 2 and 3: Break free from the past; luck comes from the modern and contemporary.

❊

A **shovel** reveals an unexpected halt in routine and warns of divided forces and greed. Sales of something old. Laying horizontally: professional advice required. Be conservative; consolidate. Blade pointing upwards: hold on; don't sell. Blade pointing down: poor health; stalemate in renovation.

❊

A **snake** warns against rash behavior

and anger. Unwelcome guests; home improvement expenses or purchases. Sector 2: Changes of opinion make for healthy outcome; go with the unplanned and spontaneous. Sectors 2 and 3: astrology; suggests secret meetings, hideaways.

The **spider** speaks of travel, retreats, and homes away from home. Favors reflection and self-improvement. Sector 2: a minor win; games of chance. Sector 3:

break free from old behavior patterns. Lighten up; enjoy healthy risks.

*

A corkscrew-like **spiral** symbolizes fertility, renewed enthusiasm, and increased vitality. In Sectors 1 and 2: news of marriage, children; new home. Sectors 2 and 3: return to business-at-hand; new job promotion.

*

A **square**—like a child's building block—symbolizes profits via slow, solid growth; demolition; out with the old. Sectors 1 and 2: health improves; success by slow and deliberate action. Sector 3: a return to nature; vacation; retire; a secret investment.

The **star**—five, six, or otherwise pointed—signifies a happy heart; good karma. Sector 1: lottery win; minor inheritance. Sector 2: luck from gut-feelings; reassuring or positive news about new friend/coworker. Sectors 2 and

3: unexpected rewards; new or extra source of income. The "fatter" the star, the bigger the happiness.

🦋

The **sun** is a thumb's up from your guardian angel; a reward for humanitarian work and consideration of others' feelings. Home improvement favored, not travel. Sectors 2 and 3: love affair; new home; education, contracts, formal negotiations, and legalities.

🦋

Beware of arguments and rash behavior warns the **sword**. A call for logic; keep both eyes open. Sector 1: debate and arguments; relationship hassles and break-ups. Sector 2 and 3: facts unclear; misguided energy. Pointing up: concludes with personal victory. Pointing downward: a pie in the face. Travel the high road.

⋙⋙⫞⫞⫞ T ⫞⫞⫞⋘⋘

The **teapot** symbolizes family peace; compromise; recuperation. Lucky for authors, poets, and musicians. Sectors 2 and 3: Financial tension eases. Always a pleasant image and reminder to phone home.

🦋

A **triangle** suggests slowing down; incomplete plans; review and reconsider; not a time for action. Don't tackle more than is healthy. Pointing upwards equals positive; answer is "yes;" opposite when pointing downwards.

🦋

A **tree** calls for strength in numbers and symbolizes unexpected welcomed assistance; renewed vigor and strength. The more lush and full the bough and foliage, the happier and healthier the end results. Make your corner of the world a better and more interesting place.

✄

The **turtle** symbolizes the home or real estate; ancestors. Common sense rules; intelligent communications amongst family members. Loans repaid; sales conclude. Sector 1: news about family elders. Sector 3: slow down and don't rush.

❧ U ❧

An open **umbrella** suggests protection; recuperation; a secret helper. An open, upside-down umbrella standing on its point says keep all cards close your chest; new plan necessary. Sector 1: Face your problem with confidence Sectors 2 and 3: help from afar.

V

vase featuring a flower or two assures
that secrets are safe; allow for a healthy
private indulgence. Sectors 1 and 3:
unexpected, helpful windfall; reserved
funds; successful backup plans. Sector
2: flirtation; the arts.

W

Pull in your markers—the cavalry arrives when the **wagon** appears.
Health-wise, proper care and diagnoses;

professional helper. Sector 2: the need for privacy. Short trips go very well. Sector 3 favors big ticket item purchases and transportation.

Wavy lines, like water, warn of deception; immature, illogical game plan. A call for sobriety. Sector 1: long-distance travel; nature-natural is the answer. Emotions overwhelm logic; intuition is "off" now. Sector 3: the need for rest and recuperation.

An old-fashioned spinning **wheel** coos look and listen. Slow, steady progress. Leave the familiar behind; experiment; wander. Sectors 1 and 2: a karmic turning point; inheritance.

A **wine glass** (or champagne flute) symbolizes celebration and joyful festivities; escape. Sector 1: party time; short trips; relax. Sector 3: warns of too much of a "good" thing.

⚒║║║ X ║║║⚒

Resembling the treasure map's "**X**,"
this symbol warns of conflicts and
arguments. Keep your own counsel;
tell no one and trust your instincts.
Sector 1: broken promises. The truth
will set you free.

SECRETS FROM A
*Tea-Leaf
Reader's Journal*

The Truth lies
in a bowl of tea.
—N. Sokeí

How to Do a "Yes-No: Reading

After the tea has finished brewing,
pour yourself a cup, clear your mind,
and, before you sip, move it in a counter-
clockwise circle three times. Or, opt
for stirring your brew with a teaspoon in three counter-clockwise
circles instead. Afterwards, take a
few calming breaths and mentally
formulate your "yes-no" query—will

he? Won't she? Should I?

Take another sip. Swirl the leaves in your cup, holding your concern in your mind. Continue this until finished. Deposit excess liquid in saucer and turn the teacup upright. In your mind's eye, divide the cup into two equal halves—using the cup-handle as a dividing line works well.

When the left-hand side of the cup features more tea leaves, your answer is "no." The cluttered, left-sided teacup proclaims this a better time for planning than action. Chill. Re-group. Retreat from the noise.

However, a teacup's busy or leaf-heavy right-side gives two thumbs up to your query and shouts, "yes, indeedy!" Go forward in confidence. The cosmos is providing you with more slack than usual.

When both the left and right sides of cup are equally embellished, the answer is "not now, kiddo." Grab a coin and flip it. Or, better yet, follow your initial gut-feeling.

Lookalike Leaves—What to Do?

Some symbols appear almost identical—like the 4-sided diamond (thinner on opposite points and wider in center), the 4-sided square (of equal length), and a 4-sided kite (like a thinner diamond with an anemic tail at one end). When in doubt, ask your intuition first, then consult the glossary.

First, look for a common factor in each symbol's definition. Like-shaped symbols often give off similar vibes, but aren't exact. Here, the diamond, square, and kite individually give off encouraging energy, suggesting positive results and forward motion. The square and diamond's energies are slow and healthy, while the kite prefers the quicker pace.

Next, note where and in what Sector each one's at. In this example, the kite—with a wisp of trailing tail—is in the middle-right part of the cup near the handle (a.k.a. Sector 2); and the diamond and square across from the cup handle and left and towards the rim.

Translation: Recent weight loss and health situations (diamond; Sector 1, a very short while ago) may have forced you to slow down at work, causing you to re-prioritize spendings (square; Sector 2, past) . . . but, all things considered, all is well right now. It was smart that you got away to re-examine your diet and reason for your stress (diamond). Use the extra money you get from buying, not selling, to get something to keep you healthy.

Travel for pleasure featuring reconnecting with faraway loved ones and some enjoyable nostalgic reunions (kite in Sector 2, rim; right-side, handle) are in your upcoming future. For the time being, start celebrating what you want to see more of, make room for fresh imaginings. Test-taking, credential-tweaking, and contract-signings will go better than hoped. It's time to start defining yourself with accounts of what you love, value, and regard as precious. Success is getting what you want Happiness is wanting what you get.

This book has been bound
using handcraft methods and
Smyth-sewn to ensure durability.

Written by Dennis Fairchild

Illustrated by Kim Scafuro

Designed by Sarah Pierson

Edited by Zachary Leibman

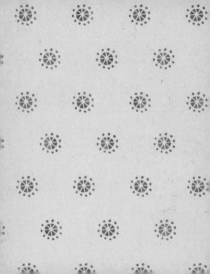